Emma

Emma Twigg's Incredible Journey to Olympic Gold

Written and Illustrated by Jessica Lawry

T0116607

Every Olympic gold medal begins with a dream.

For Emma Twigg, her dream of gold started as a girl in the Hawke's Bay,
as she watched, spellbound, her Olympic heroes competing to win.

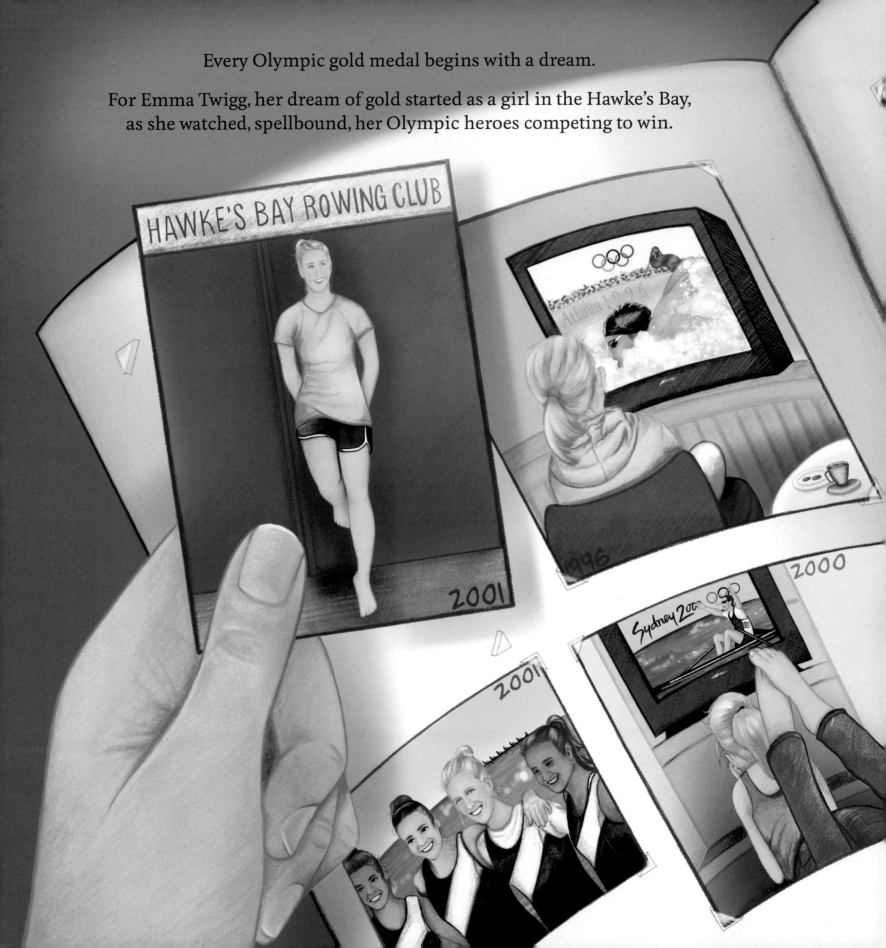

Emma decided to give rowing a go.

She started out as part of a team of keen schoolgirls in a heavy wooden boat, with old slides and large spoon paddles.

It was hard work, and it wasn't always fun.

Summertime weekends were spent at regattas with her team in the blistering sun, rowing one race after another.

At club national competitions, Emma met her heroes — the inspirational gold medallists she had watched at the Olympics as she was growing up.

Emma found that she was catching the
rowing bug.

Determined to carve her own way in the
sport, she decided to become a single sculler.

She started to work tirelessly, alone.

Rowing away the hours on hot summer days, Emma trained on Hawkes Bay's Clive River, until the dark crept along the river banks and over the water.

Her muscles ached, her body groaned.

Determined, confident and headstrong, Emma set her sights on the World Rowing Championships and the Beijing 2008 Olympic Games.

She gathered together her team: friends, parents, coach.

She moved to Cambridge in the Waikato, the centre of rowing excellence in New Zealand.

Emma kept training, sometimes rowing up to 200 km a week.

And then the day came when Emma got the call: at just 21 years old, she was off to her first Olympic Games.

She fizzed!

Her family and friends celebrated with her. The dream of chasing a gold medal was now within reach.

In Beijing, the Olympic village was mind-blowing: bright lights, huge spaces, important people. Many, many heroes. Emma felt overjoyed, it really was a dream come true!

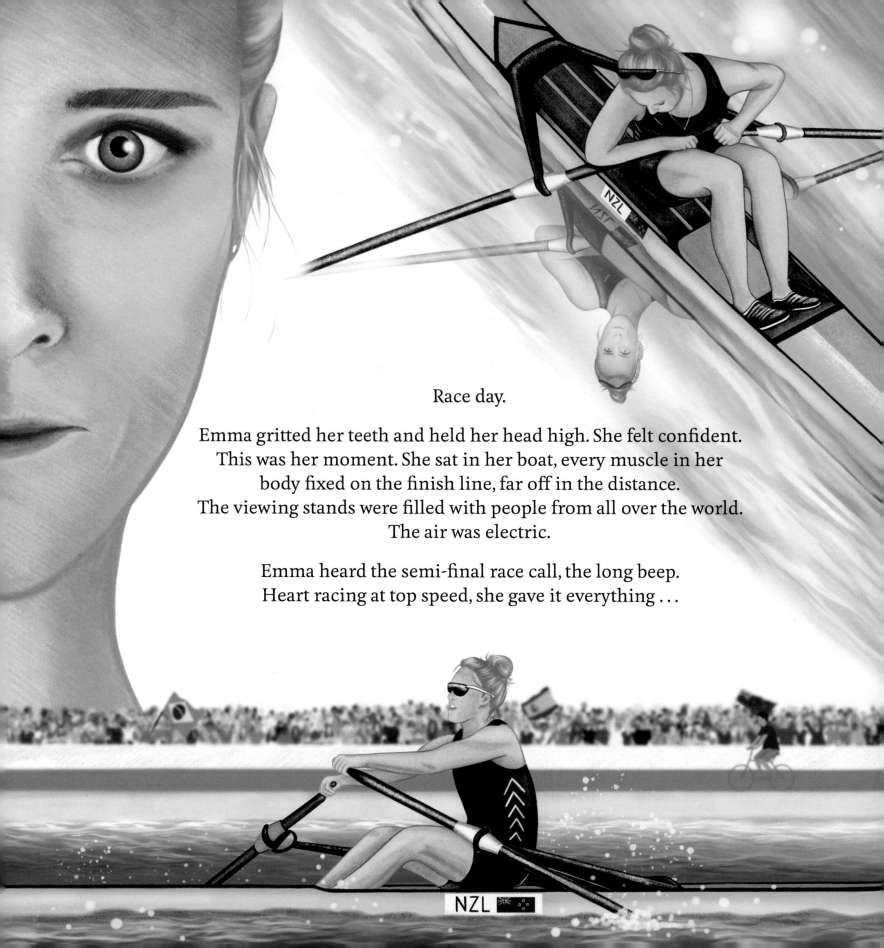

Race day.

Emma gritted her teeth and held her head high. She felt confident.
This was her moment. She sat in her boat, every muscle in her
body fixed on the finish line, far off in the distance.
The viewing stands were filled with people from all over the world.
The air was electric.

Emma heard the semi-final race call, the long beep.
Heart racing at top speed, she gave it everything . . .

Fourth place.

Emma felt pain right through her body. She had missed out on the medal race!
Frustrated and disappointed, Emma knew she hadn't shown the
world what she knew she could do.

Why had she expected it to be easy?

After returning home and taking time to recover,
there was only one thing for it.
Emma's gold medal dream lived on,
and she had to get back into the sport she knew so well.

Back to the boat, back to the water, back to the training hours
and the calluses all over her hands.

On crisp mornings at Lake Karāpiro, there would be Emma,
quietly gliding through the water.

Emma would listen to the rhythm of her oars cutting into the water and the
bubbles running under the hull. Every morning the coaching boat motor
hummed alongside her, sometimes muffled by the fresh morning fog,
and on other days silenced by the sound of heavy rain.

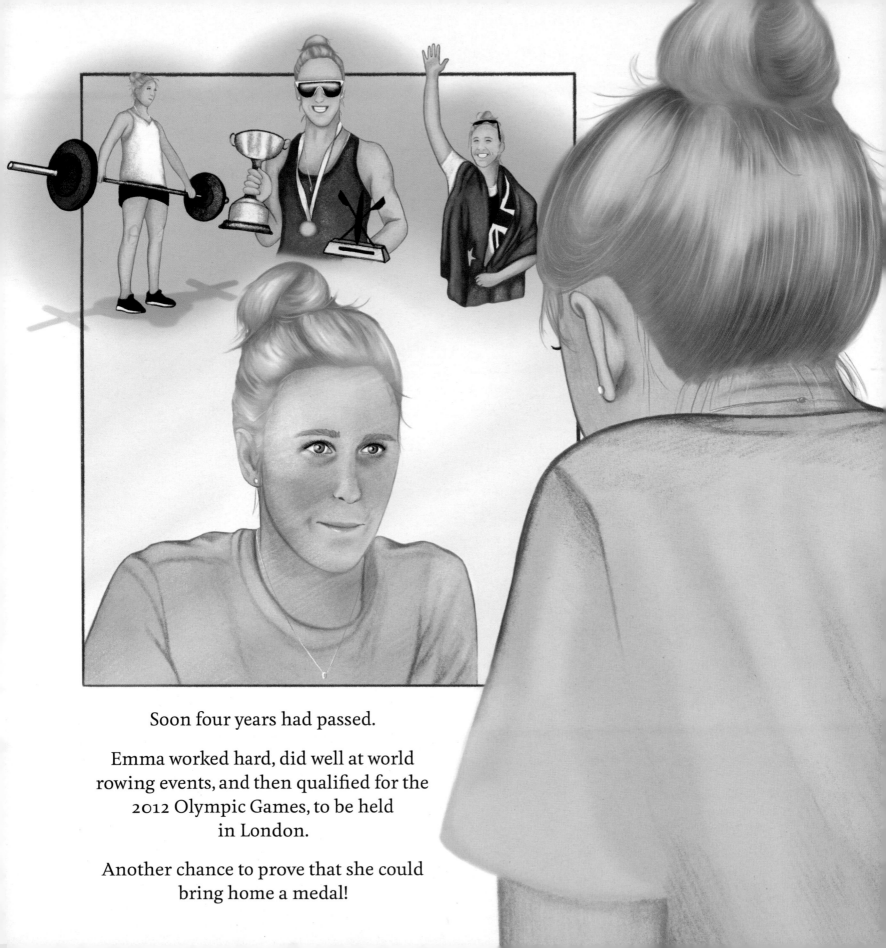

Soon four years had passed.

Emma worked hard, did well at world rowing events, and then qualified for the 2012 Olympic Games, to be held in London.

Another chance to prove that she could bring home a medal!

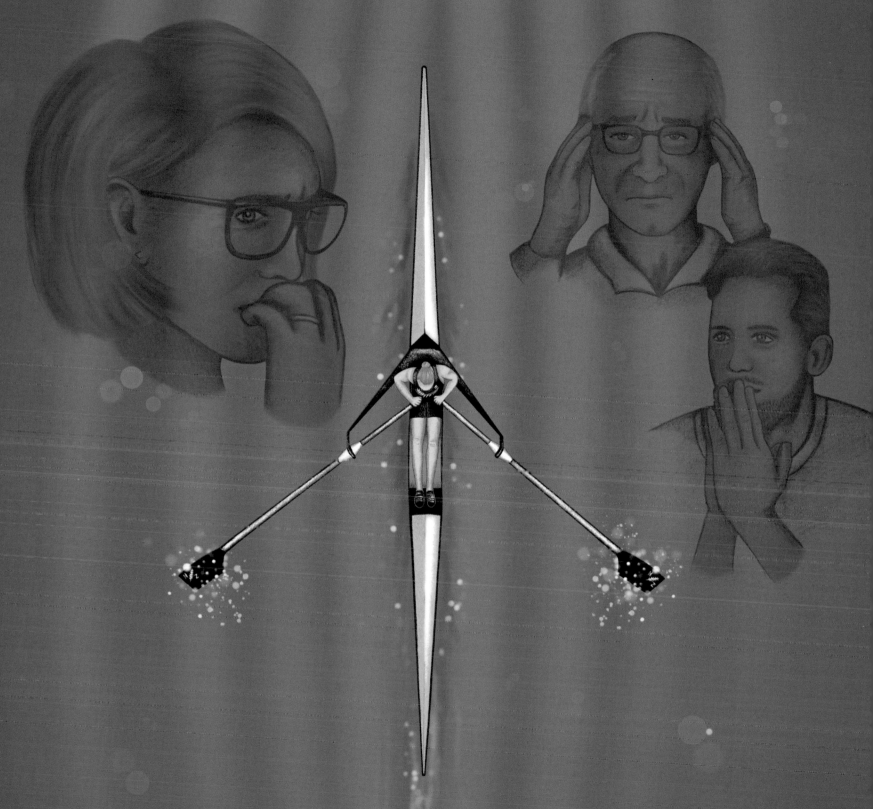

On Dorney Lake, her 2012 Olympic stage, Emma rowed herself into the final. Her support team were on the edge of their seats. The familiar long beep to start the race echoed around her. **"Push!"** she yelled at herself.

Fourth place.
Three seconds from a medal.

Enough was enough. That was it.
Emma put away her oars and left the boat.
She needed to take some time out.

Taking a break was a chance for Emma to think about her life and her goals. Emma travelled and studied. She met new people, made new friends. She realised she was liked for who she was, not because she wore a medal.

Emma was free of the pressure, but not free of the question — next time, could she bring a medal home?

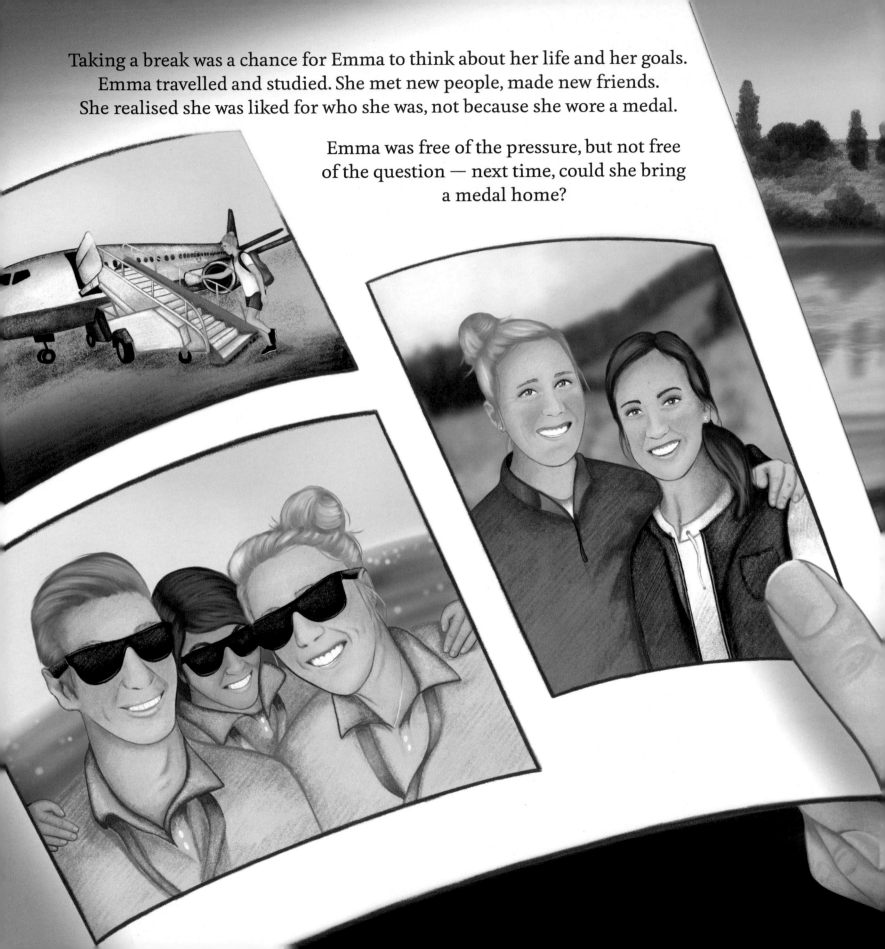

Emma came home to Cambridge, and got back into the boat.
The hard work resumed. In a whirlwind she won the
Last Chance Regatta, and qualified for the
Rio de Janeiro 2016 Olympic Games.

In the final at Rio, Emma lined up against her long-standing rivals.

Was this her moment at last?
She saw her support team watching in the crowd.
Her name blasted over the speaker, then came the long beep.

Emma emptied herself on the water that day.
There was simply nothing left.

Fourth again, by just a sliver of a second.

Brave, although broken, Emma smiled and waved to her team.

They had been there with her through thick and thin. They were her village, and she loved them.

Emma decided that was it, she was done.

She walked away. Away from fifteen years
of hard work, away from the pressure,
away from the sport she held so close to her heart.

Emma walked away from her Olympic dream.

Once again, Emma worked overseas and tried new things. Her father had told her to "do what makes you happy, and the rest of life will figure itself out."

She knew she really loved to row. She missed the purpose she felt when she was on the water. She still wanted to do well at the Olympics, not just for the shiny medal, but to prove to herself that she was better than her past performances.

But time was running out.

Returning home, Emma's team was happy to see her.
Their support for Emma was unfaltering, but there was a lot of work to do.

Emma realised that she was already surrounded by gold, with the support of those who helped
her to see how much she could learn from her times at the Olympics.
They gave her the gift of belief.

Covid-19 arrived, pushing the 2020 Olympic Games in Tokyo to 2021. It was a long five years
between the Olympic Games. Emma's team increased to include many experts,
her long-supporting friends and family, and other Olympic athletes, too.

Emma trained harder than ever. Her life became: rowing,
eating and resting . . . and rowing some more.

Emma's team had her back for every rowing stroke,
and the strength of their belief in Emma powered her growing belief in herself,
in her boat, body and mind, and what she could do.

Race day at the Tokyo Olympic Games.

Emma pinched herself. Despite the pandemic, she had made it to Tokyo. And she was about to race! Emma was ready, more ready than ever before.

She set her mind on steady, deep breathing. Her chest rose and fell. The sweat dripped from her forehead. Not a sound disturbed her focus.

Tokyo's Sea Forest Waterway was still. There were no crowds, just a small masked group of other athletes.

The familiar long beep sounded, a green light.

Emma dug deep. Deeper, and deeper still.
She dug hard into the water, and into her self-belief.
Her mind was clear. Every time she leaned into a stroke,
she also leaned on her team and everything that she had learned
every time she had rowed a race.
She moved through the water with speed, strength and finesse.
She owned the race.

Breaking the finish line . . .

GOLD!

It was a clean win, and an Olympic record!

After twenty years of sacrifice, she had done it: for her country, with her team.
Emma joined her heroes as an Olympic champion. It was the best feeling imaginable.

She turned to her team, her face glowing. There were smiles, tears, and pure . . . joy.

Emma now had her gold medal. Her Olympic dream had finally come true. But she
had an even greater gift: the gold she had found on her journey to the medal.

Jessica lives with her husband and three children in the Waikato, New Zealand. When she is not writing or illustrating, she is a primary school teacher and loves to travel and do anything creative. She met Emma while studying at Waikato University, and has followed Emma's incredible rowing career since. When Emma won the gold medal at the Tokyo Olympics in 2021, Jessica felt compelled to write and illustrate Emma's story for its inspirational value and teachings of resilience and perseverance for young readers. *Emma* is her first picture book.

For Matt, Max, Stella and Neve for their unfaltering love and support and for the friends and family that helped make my dream come true — J.L

Emma lives with her wife and son in the Waikato, New Zealand. When she is not rowing, Emma enjoys spending time with family and friends. Emma wanted to share her career highs and lows with Kiwi kids in picture book format as she staunchly believes in inspiring the next generation. Emma also wanted to communicate the importance of teamwork, hard work and perseverance for kids who have a goal in any aspect of their lives.

For my team, especially Char and Tommy — E.T

A catalogue record for this book is available from the National Library of New Zealand

ISBN 978-1-990003-64-6

An Upstart Press Book
Published in 2022 by Upstart Press Ltd
26 Greeenpark Road, Penrose,
Auckland 1061, New Zealand

Text © Emma Twigg and Jessica Lawry 2022
Illustrations © Jessica Lawry 2022
The moral right of the author has been asserted.
Design and format © Upstart Press Ltd 2022

All rights reserved. No part of this publication may be reproduced or transmitted in any form or by any means, electronic or mechanical, including photocopying, recording, or any information storage and retrieval system, without permission in writing from the publisher.

Olympic content approved by the New Zealand Olympic Committee.
Photography by Katie Hurlow Photography, www.katiehurlow.com.
Designed by Nick Turzynski, redinc. book design, www.redinc.co.nz
Printed by 1010 Printing International Ltd., China